Published in Great Britain in 1986
by Exley Publications Ltd,
16 Chalk Hill, Watford,
Herts WD1 4BN, United Kingdom.
Second printing October 1988

Selection and design © Exley Publications, 1986

ISBN 1-85015-067-2

Printed and bound in Hungary.

Thank heavens for friends!

Edited by Helen Exley

FRIENDS!

It is a good thing to be rich, and a good thing to be strong, but it is a better thing to be beloved of many friends.

Euripides

Friendship is unnecessary, like philosophy, like art ... It has no survival value; rather it is one of those things that give value to survival.

C.S. Lewis

Who seeks a friend without a fault remains without one.

Proverb from the Turkish

Go often to the house of thy friend; for weeds soon choke up the unused path.

Edda [Scandinavian Mythology]

One does not make friends; one recognizes them.

Isabel Paterson

I don't need a friend who changes when I change and who nods when I nod; my shadow does that much better.

Plutarch

God gave us our relatives: thank God we can choose our friends.

Ethel Watts Mumford

DEFINITIONS OF FRIENDSHIP

The most I can do for my friend is simply to be
his friend. I have no wealth to bestow on him.
If he knows that I am happy in loving him, he
will want no other reward. Is not friendship
divine in this?   *Henry David Thoreau*

A friend is the one who comes in when the whole
world has gone out.   *Alban Goodier*

Treat your friends as you do your pictures, and
place them in their best light.

Jennie Jerome Churchill

Nothing more dangerous than a friend without
discretion; even a prudent enemy is preferable.

Jean de la Fontaine

The making of friends, who are real friends, is
the best token we have of a person's success in
life.   *Edward Everett Hale*

Do not save your loving speeches
For your friends till they are dead;
Do not write them on their tombstones,
Speak them rather now instead.

Anna Cummins

A FRIEND IS ...

A friend is one who incessantly pays us the compliment of expecting from us all the virtues, and who can appreciate them in us.

The friend asks no return but that his friend will religiously accept and wear and not disgrace his apotheosis of him. They cherish each other's hopes. They are kind to each other's dreams.

That kindness which has so good a reputation elsewhere can least of all consist with this relation, and no such affront can be offered to a friend, as a conscious good-will, a friendliness which is not a necessity of the friend's nature.

Friendship is never established as an understood relation. It is a miracle which requires constant proofs. It is an exercise of the purest imagination and of the rarest faith.

We do not wish for friends to feed and clothe our bodies – neighbors are kind enough for that – but to do the life office to our spirit. For this, few are rich enough, however well disposed they may be ....

The language of friendship is not words, but meanings. It is an intelligence above language.

Henry David Thoreau

A FRIEND

A friend is a present you give yourself.

Robert Louis Stevenson

I no doubt deserved my enemies, but I don't believe I deserved my friends.

Walt Whitman

If two people who love each other let a single instant wedge itself between them, it grows – it becomes a month, a year, a century; it becomes too late.

Jean Giraudoux

I do not wish to treat friendships daintily, but with roughest courage. When they are real, they are not glass threads or frost-work, but the solidest thing we know.

Ralph Waldo Emerson

The holy passion of friendship is so sweet and steady and loyal and enduring a nature that it will last through a whole lifetime, if not asked to lend money.

Mark Twain

… when people have light in themselves, it will shine out from them. Then we get to know each other as we walk together in the darkness, without needing to pass our hands over each other's faces, or to intrude into each other's hearts.

Albert Schweitzer

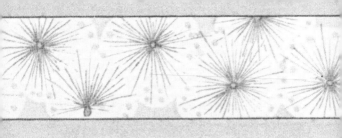

from "THE PROPHET"

And a youth said, Speak to us of Friendship.
And he answered, saying:
Your friend is your needs answered.
He is your field which you sow with love and
    reap with thanksgiving.
And he is your board and your fireside.
For you come to him with your hunger, and
    you seek him for peace.

When your friend speaks his mind you fear not
    the "nay" in your own mind, nor do you with-
    hold the "ay".
And when he is silent your heart ceases not to
    listen to his heart;
For without words, in friendship, all thoughts,
    all desires, all expectations are born and
    shared, with joy that is unacclaimed.
When you part from your friend, you grieve not;
For that which you love most in him may be
    clearer in his absence, as the mountain to the

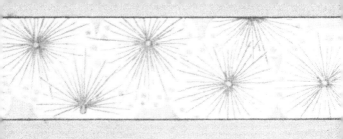

climber is clearer from the plain.
And let there be no purpose in friendship save
the deepening of the spirit.
For love that seeks aught but the disclosure of
its own mystery is not love but a net cast forth:
and only the unprofitable is caught.

And let your best be for your friend.
If he must know the ebb of your tide, let him
know its flood also.
For what is your friend that you should seek him
with hours to kill?
Seek him always with hours to live.
For it is his to fill your need, but not your
emptiness.
And in the sweetness of friendship let there be
laughter, and sharing of pleasures.
For in the dew of little things the heart finds
its morning and is refreshed.

Kahlil Gibran, "The Prophet"

THE GIFT OF FRIENDSHIP

I know now that the world is not filled with
strangers. It is full of other people – waiting only
to be spoken to.   *Beth Day*

... to find a friend one must close one eye: to
keep him, two.   *Norman Douglas*

First of all things, for friendship, there must be
that delightful, indefinable state called feeling
at ease with your companion, – the one man,
the one woman out of a multitude who interests
you, who meets your thoughts and tastes.
                                              Julia Duhring

Anybody can sympathize with the sufferings of
a friend, but it requires a very fine nature to
sympathize with a friend's success.
                                              Oscar Wilde

But of all plagues, good Heaven, thy wrath can
    send,
Save me, oh, save me, from the candid friend.
                                              George Canning

Instead of loving your enemies, treat your
friends a little better.   *Edgar Watson Howe*

MISCELLANEOUS FILE

Just why should friends be chronological,
Fraternal friends, or pedagogical,
Alike in race or taste or color –
It only makes the meetings duller!
Unclassified by tribe or steeple,
Why shouldn't friends be merely people?

Dorothy Brown Thompson

Little friends may prove great friends.

Aesop

WITHOUT A WORD, WITHOUT A SIGN

I love you not only for what you are,
but for what I am when I am with you.

I love you not only for what you have made
of yourself, but for what you are making of me.

I love you because you have done more than
   any creed
could have done to make me good, and more
than any fate could have done to make me happy.

You have done it without a touch,
without a word, without a sign.

You have done it by being yourself. Perhaps
that is what being a friend means, after all.

Anonymous

WHEN SILENCE IS BEYOND WORDS

There may be moments in friendship, as in love,
when silence is beyond words. The faults of our
friend may be clear to us, but it is well to seem
to shut our eyes to them. Friendship is usually
treated by the majority of people as a tough and
everlasting thing which will survive all manner

of bad treatment. But this is an exceedingly great and foolish error; it may die in an hour of a single unwise word; its conditions of existence are that it should be dealt with delicately and tenderly, being as it is a sensible plant and not a roadside thistle. We must not expect our friend to be above humanity.

Ouida

SOUNDING-BOARD

What is a friend to me? In the simplest terms, it's someone who will allow me to be the way I am and not think me totally round the bend. Someone who can tell by the look on my face when I need to talk about what's happening, or not happening, in my life. Someone who provides non-judgmental support. It is extremely therapeutic to have the opportunity to discuss problems, to consider possibilities, to use friends as a sounding-board, in order to see your problems differently. A friend is someone who needs me, trusts me, and is happy when my news is good; someone who won't go away.

I was brought up to be Miss Priss, Miss Shockable. But I was also brought up to challenge my values. My parents taught me that the world may take your money, your home, your livelihood ... so what? Friends should be treasured. And to have good friends, you must *be* a good friend. That's what mother told me. As always, she was right.

Angela Douglas

... AGAINST ALL THE EVILS OF LIFE

Life is to be fortified by many friendships. To
love, and to be loved, is the greatest happiness.
If I lived under the burning sun of the equator,
it would be pleasure for me to think that there
were many human beings on the other side of
the world who regarded and respected me; I
could not live if I were alone upon the earth,
and cut off from the remembrance of my fellow-
creatures. It is not that a person has occasion
often to fall back upon the kindness of friends;
perhaps we may never experience the necessity
of doing so; but we are governed by our
imaginations, and they stand there as a solid and
impregnable bulwark against all the evils of life.

Sydney Smith

RED-LETTER DAYS

There are red-letter days in our lives when we meet people who thrill us like a fine poem, people whose handshake is brimful of unspoken sympathy and whose sweet, rich natures impart to our eager, impatient spirits a wonderful restfulness .... Perhaps we never saw them before and they may never cross our life's path again; but the influence of their calm, mellow natures is a libation poured upon our discontent, and we feel its healing touch as the ocean feels the mountain stream freshening its brine ....

Helen Keller

His thoughts were slow,
His words were few, and never formed to glisten.
But he was a joy to all his friends –
You should have heard him listen.

– quoted by Wayne Mackey in Oklahoma City Times

Someone long parted from us can recognise us,
despite all the changes that the years have
brought. We are ourselves, unique and known.
We feed upon the years, our natures modified
by each experience, but never changed beyond
all recognition. Pain, loss, all the dark things
existence can impose, cannot destroy us.

Charlotte Gray

"YOU HAVEN'T CHANGED AT ALL!"

Time peels and patches, plumps out and pares away
all that we were, and yet, one day,
someone we've passed, unseeing, in the street
will turn and gasp and greet
us as if all the years,
the struggles and the failures and the tears
had left us quite unmarked. And they will say
"It's you! You haven't changed at all!"
(And suddenly you both are four feet tall
and thin and shy: and know that it is true.
We are the same as then.)
"My dear! And nor have you!"

Pam Brown

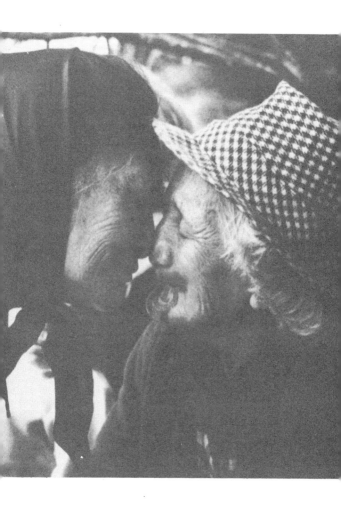

ANOTHER SPRING

Friendships fail some years,
blight twists the leaves and the crop is bitter.
Frost bites
or sudden fire devours:
but the root lies sound
and waits for better weather
or a storm of sleet to scour the branches.
Then we shall see another spring:
a flare of green flame
and flowers burning to fruit
along the boughs.

Charlotte Gray

WHEN YOU DON'T EDIT YOURSELF

A friend is someone to whom you can say any jackass thing that enters your mind. With acquaintances, you are forever aware of their slightly unreal image of you, and you edit yourself to fit. Many marriages are between acquaintances. You can be with a person for three hours of your life and have a friend. Another one will remain an acquaintance for thirty years.

J.D. MacDonald

FRIENDSHIP IS ...

It is a sweet thing, friendship, a dear balm,
A happy and auspicious bird of calm,
Which rides o'er life's ever tumultuous Ocean;
A god that broods o'er chaos in commotion;
A flower which fresh as Lapland roses are,
Lifts its bold head into the world's frore air,
And blooms most radiantly when others die,
Health, hope, and youth, and brief prosperity;

And with the light and odour of its bloom,
Shining within the dungeon and the tomb;
Whose coming is as light and music are
'Mid dissonance and gloom – a star
Which moves not 'mid the moving heavens alone –
A smile among dark frowns – a gentle tone
Among rude voices, a beloved light,
A solitude, a refuge, a delight.

Percy Bysshe Shelley

SMALL SERVICE

Small service is true service while it lasts;
Of friends, however humble, scorn not one;
The daisy, by the shadow that it casts,
Protects the lingering dewdrop from the sun.

William Wordsworth

Oh, the comfort, the inexpressible comfort, of feeling safe with a person; having neither to weigh thoughts nor measure words, but to pour them all out just as they are, chaff and grain together, knowing that a faithful hand will take and sift them, keep what is worth keeping, and then, with the breath of kindness, blow the rest away.

George Eliot

The friends thou hast, and their adoption tried,
Grapple them to thy soul with hoops of steel;
But do not dull thy palm with entertainment
Of each new-hatch'd, unfledg'd comrade. Beware
Of entrance to a quarrel; but being in,
Bear't that th'opposed may beware of thee.
Give every man thine ear, but few thy voice;
Take each man's censure, but reserve thy
    judgment...
Neither a borrower, nor a lender be;
For loan oft loses itself and friend,
And borrowing dulls the edge of husbandry.
This above all: to thine own self be true,
And it must follow, as the night the day,
Thou canst not then be false to any man.

William Shakespeare

SURPRISES FROM DEVIZES

Friends bring you back surprises
from Devizes:

Not rock or pots of clotted cream,
but something that you once remarked in passing
you coveted with all your heart,
and then forgot.
Friends carry lists inside their heads
of chance remarks
and little loving looks.
They swoop
at sales
and bear away in triumph something that you lack
as if it is their trophy
and not yours.
They fill the gaps
in uneventful living,
stuff flowers along the cracks of concrete
over which we tread.
They patch the days with kindness
and accept
our gestures of affection,
windfalls and scones and pots of bramble jam
with equal joy
to ours.
Friends stitch the world together.

Pam Brown

from "A CHILD'S VIEW OF HAPPINESS"

Happiness is if you give it away.

Christopher Hoare, 11

Happiness is giving a little and taking a little,
even if it is a mere dandelion. It is worth a
bouquet of red roses wrapped in delicate lace if
it is given with care. *Helen Caddick, 11*

I like to see the persons face light up with joy,
and the rustling of the wrapping paper being
torn off of the present. It's so nice when they
thank you for the present, and that warms you
all over. *Paul Owen, 13*

Karen Thomson, 5

Happiness is my friend's hand.

Gillian Queen, 10

Happiness is the whole world as friends. It's
light all through your life.

Daniel Dilling, 8

Happiness is like a disease. It spreads.

Simon Elliot, 11

It costs nothing to say a "hello" here and there.
To friends that you pass in the street.
It costs nothing to smile at a stranger,
Or at any new friend that you meet.
It costs nothing to show your emotions,
or your feelings when things don't go right.
It costs nothing to help the unfortunate,
Who are blind or who have no sight.
It costs nothing to be happy.
And happiness can be found.
Happiness is like butter,
So go on and spread some around.

Jeanette Achilles, 15

Some people have a beautiful smile and when
people see it they feel happy.

Susannah Morris, 10

WITHOUT FRIENDS

Without friends no one would choose to live,
though he had all other goods; even rich people,
and those in possession of office and of
dominating power are thought to need friends
most of all; for what is the use of such prosperity
without the opportunity of beneficence, which
is exercised chiefly and in its most laudable form
towards friends? Or how can prosperity be
guarded and preserved without friends? The
greater it is, the more exposed is it to risk. And
in poverty and in other misfortunes people think
friends are the only refuge. It helps the young,
too, to keep from error; it aids older people by
ministering to their needs and supplementing
the activities that are failing from weakness;
those in the prime of life it stimulates to noble
actions ... for with friends people are more able
both to think and to act.

Aristotle

WHAT IS A FRIEND?

Friends don't even notice the body you are living in.

I once knew I was going to be friends with a family before I even met them: they moved into the empty house up the road, and called it "Fred".

Friends are people who go on conspiratorial shopping sprees together, diving in and out of shops totally beyond their price range, and ending up eating oozing cream cakes with only just enough money to get home.

Friends don't actually lie for each other – but they put down very good smoke screens.

A friend never mentions a *thing* to old blabbermouth over the road.

Everyone half hopes there's a heaven – just to put things right with old friends.

Acquaintances call nervously to ask if they can do anything to help. Friends come and sit with your horribly infectious kids while you dash off to the Denver conert.

Friends don't have to be good looking or sexy – come to think of it, maybe that's why they are friends.

Love is blind; friendship quietly closes its eyes.

A friend is the one person who can correct your faults – and has the sense not to try.

A friendship can be made in ten minutes ... even if you never see each other again, you are now part of each other's lives forever.

It's easier to love mankind than keep a few friendships in good repair.

Love links two lives inextricably, like Siamese twins. Friendship lets you walk comfortably side by side.

Pam Brown

BOUND TO US IN TRIUMPH AND DISASTER

On the level of the human spirit an equal, a
companion, an understanding heart is one who
can share a person's point of view. What this
means we all know. Friends, companions,
lovers, are those who treat us in terms of our
unlimited worth to ourselves. They are closest
to us who best understand what life means to
us, who feel for us as we feel for ourselves, who
are bound to us in triumph and disaster, who
break the spell of our loneliness.

Henry Alonzo Myers

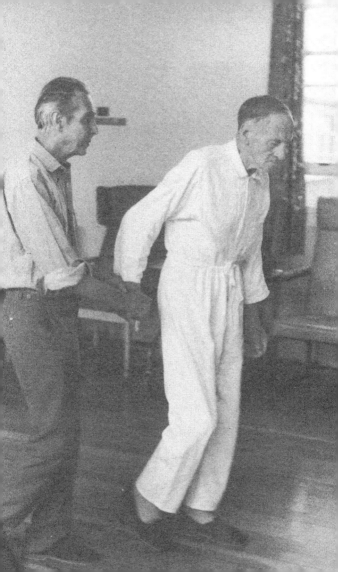

A SORROW SHARED

If a friend of mine ... gave a feast, and did not
invite me to it, I should not mind a bit .... But
if ... a friend of mine had a sorrow and refused
to allow me to share it, I should feel it most
bitterly. If a friend shut the doors of the house
of mourning against me, I would move back
again and again and beg to be admitted so that
I might share in what I was entitled to share. If
my friend thought me unworthy, unfit to weep
with him, I should feel it as the most poignant
humiliation ....

Oscar Wilde

PEOPLE NEED PEOPLE

In Munich there was a grim, boring apartment block where there were problems of loneliness and distrust. People didn't talk much to neighbours – a lot like tall tower blocks everywhere.

Photographer Peter Nemetschek, shocked by the cold, inhuman look of the building, took photos of the tenants and hung them, poster size, in their windows.

Soon the people began talking to people living near them, people on the top floor recognized faces on the first floor and invited them up for coffee. Neighbours became friends; not just another face and flat number.

Dalton Harold

"HE'S ALIVE!"

Two miners in a mine in New Mexico had placed eleven charges of dynamite at the bottom of an eighty-five-foot shaft, and prepared their fuses with enough time to scramble up to the higher levels, where they would be protected from the blast. Then things went terrifyingly wrong. With the fuses burning, the first miner, Carl Myers, reached safety. But before his mate Harry Reid reached the protected area, one of the charges went off. Harry was punched down by the blast, knocked unconscious, wounded by hundreds of splinters driven into his legs. Carl called frantically. No reply. And the rest of those sticks of dynamite were seconds away from exploding, with certain death for Harry. Carl hurled himself back down the slope again, gathered his unconscious friend onto his back and started to claw his way back up the slope to safety, every sinew in his body pounding under the strain, every second ticking in his brain. As he reached the top – and collapsed to safety – the dynamite ripped the mountain. The company Carl and Harry worked for wanted to sponsor Carl for the Carnegie Award for Heroism. Carl was having none of it. "Damn the medal," he muttered. "He's alive, isn't he?"

Richard Alan

"I learnt that man does not live by care for himself, but by love for others. It was not given the mother to know what was needful for the life of her children; it was not given to the rich man to know what was needful for himself; and it is not given to any man to know whether by the evening he will want boots for his living body or slippers for his corpse. When I came to earth as a man, I lived not by care for myself, but by the love that was in the heart of a passer-by, and his wife, and because they were kind and merciful to me. The orphans lived not by any care they had for themselves; they lived through the love that was in the heart of a stranger, a woman who was kind and merciful to them. *And all people live, not by reason of any care they have for themselves, but by the love for them that is in other people.*

"I knew before that God gives life to men, and desires them to live; but now I know far more. I know that God does not desire men to live apart from each other, and therefore has not revealed to them what is needful for each of them to live by himself. He wishes them to live together united, and therefore has revealed to them that they are needful to each other's happiness."

Leo Tolstoy

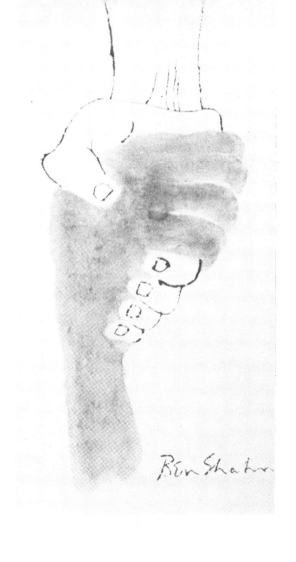

THIS <u>PARTICULAR</u> PERSON MATTERS

It is a mistake to think that one makes a friend because of his or her qualities, it has nothing to do with qualities at all. It is the person that we want, not what he does or says, or does not do or say, but what he or she *is* that is eternally enough! Who shall explain the extraordinary instinct that tells us, perhaps after a single meeting, that this or that particular person in

some mysterious way matters to us? I confess that, for myself, I never enter a new company without the hope that I may discover a friend, perhaps *the* friend, sitting there with an expectant smile. That hope survives a thousand disappointments. People who deal with life generously and large-heartedly go on multiplying relationships to the end.

Arthur Christopher Benson

ANNIE AND EDITH

Annie and Edith had known each other from the time when their skinny adolescent bodies were packed and laced and buttoned into their black, bustled frocks and their bony little feet crammed into button-hooked boots. Annie became cook to a lord, and Edith the wife of a Guardsman, to which positions they brought the gusto and doggedness and shrewd, pawky humour of their kind. Annie was the more volatile, having French blood, and frequently left home, with no ill effects to her family, as they knew quite well where she was. She was with Edith, getting it all out of her system and drinking quantities of strong tea.

Widowed, they got the weeping over with and tore even more ferociously into living. Edith took to Speedway, Annie to the Horses. Annie still left home at regular intervals, and the two of them went on minor rampages to the seaside, the black-eyed Annie and the china-blue-eyed Edith out for the day. Cockles, whelks, shrimp teas, milk stout and a little jay walking. Any guardian angels they may have had sweated as they wove their way among the crowds, crossing roads against the lights and giving young policemen lip. They never became the least drunk or disorderly. They simply had a very

good time, frequently ending up adopted by teenagers out on the spree, being fed rock salmon and chips, and allowed to sit on the motorbikes.

They were grandmas to be relished, for they had about them a rollicking, piratical air that other grans had not.

Edith died first, indignant at eighty-two to find herself suddenly old. It was a raggle-taggle funeral with all manner of unexpected people turning up, and unexpected things going wrong. Engineered, one suspected, by Edith.

Annie looked paler and more French than ever. Dressed in tight black, she wept for her ancient ally, unnerved by this abrupt silence, this assumption of dignity.

She did not last long afterwards. Ordinary people were too dull to detain her.

God knows what the pair of them are up to now.

Pam Brown

DAY OR NIGHT

What have I got for you, my friend?
The last flowers from a winter garden, to
shine against the dark. The recipe you asked for.
An envelope of seeds. An empty perfume bottle
for your little girl. A slice of cold bread pudding.
A glossy magazine, found on a train. Scones hot
from the oven. Jam hot from the stove. A small
striped kitten if you want him. An armchair past
its prime, to lend a little comfort to your son's
first home. A glass of wine. A dab of scent. Half
a box of bedding plants.
A pair of hands, a mop and comfort when
the washing machine runs berserk.
A back to brace the wardrobe you intend to
shift.
A shoulder very like your mom's to cry on.
The episode of a soap you missed, in total
recall.
Coffee.
First aid.
An extension of your own vocabulary in times
of indignation.
News of the local otter.
Availability. Day or night.

Pam Brown

OLD FRIENDS

Old friends are the great blessing of one's latter
years. Half a word conveys one's meaning. They
have a memory of the same events, and have the
same mode of thinking. I have young relations
that may grow upon me, for my nature is
affectionate, but can they grow old friends?

Horace Walpole

OLD COATS, OLD FRIENDS

My coat and I live comfortably together. It has
assumed all my wrinkles, does not hurt me
anywhere, has moulded itself on my deformities,
and is complacent to all my movements, and I
only feel its presence because it keeps me warm.
Old coats and old friends are the same thing.

Victor Hugo

NO MAN IS AN ISLAND

No man is an island, entire of itself; every man
is a piece of the continent, a part of the main.
If a clod be washed away by the sea, Europe is
the less, as well as if a promontory were, as well
as if a manor of thy friend's or of thine own
were: any man's death diminishes me, because
I am involved in mankind, and therefore never
send to know for whom the bell tolls; it tolls for
thee.

John Donne

IRISH TOASTS

May the frost never afflict your spuds.
May the outside leaves of your cabbage
always be free from worms.
May the crows never pick your haystack,
and may your donkey always be in foal.

Health and long life to you:
The husband of your choice to you.
A child every year to you.
Land without rent to you.
And may you be half-an-hour in heaven
before the devil knows you're dead.
*Sláinte!

May you live as long as you want
and never want as long as you live!

May you die in bed at 95 years,
shot by a jealous wife.

May you have warm words on a cold evening,
a full moon on a dark night,
and a smooth road all the way to your door.

May the road rise to meet you.
May the wind be always at your back,
the sun shine warm upon your face,
the rain fall soft upon your fields,
and until we meet again
may God hold you in the hollow of His hand.

from "Sláinte!"

* *Health*

The two old men
Sit in silence together,
Living in dim memories
Of the past.
They are lifelong friends
And need no words
To share their thoughts.

One quavers to the other;
"May you live a hundred years,
And may I live ninety-nine."

The other nods his old white head
And gravely says;
"Let us go home together
And drink a cup of wine."

Hsu Chi, Sung Dynasty

The cottage goes round the curved creek;
Bamboos follow the bend of the mountain.
Streams and mountains are still there
In the midst of white clouds.
Come to the creek and free the skiff;
Sit here with your back to the mountain.
With the river birds and mountain flowers,
Share my leisure.

Wang An-Shih, 1021-1086 A.D.

A KIND OF HABIT

As widowers proverbially marry again, so a man
with the habit of friendship always finds new
friends ... My old age judges more charitably
and thinks better of mankind than my youth
ever did. I discount idealization, I forgive
onesidedness. I see that it is essential to
perfection of any kind. And in each person I
catch the fleeting suggestion of something
beautiful, and swear eternal friendship with that.

George Santayana

ACKNOWLEDGEMENTS: The publishers gratefully acknowledge permission to reproduce copyright material. Every effort has been made to trace copyright holders, but in a few cases this has proved impossible. The publishers would be interested to hear from any copyright holders not here acknowledged.

RICHARD BACH, extract from *There's No Such Place As Far Away*. Reprinted with permission of Grafton Books, a division of the Collins Publishing Group and Dell Publishing, New York; PAM BROWN, "Surprises from Devizes", "Day or Night", "Annie and Edith", "You Haven't Changed At All", "What is a Friend?" definitions; DOROTHY BROWN THOMPSON, extract from *The Kansas City Star,* reprinted with permission of The Kansas City Star Co.; ANGELA DOUGLAS, "Sounding Board". Extract from an article in *She* magazine, June 1985. Reprinted with permission of John Farquharson Ltd; NANCY EBERLE, "Between Then and Now". From an article in *Glamour* magazine, July 1978. Reprinted courtesy *Glamour*. Copyright © 1978 by The Conde Nast Publications Inc; ROBERT FROST, "A Time To Talk", from *The Poetry of Robert Frost*, edited by Edward Connery Latham. Copyright 1916 © 1969 by Holt Rinehart and Winston. Copyright 1944 by Robert Frost. Reprinted by permission of Henry Holt and Company and the Estate of Robert Frost; KAHLIL GIBRAN, "On Friendship". Reprinted from *The Prophet*, by Kahlil Gibran, by permission of Alfred A. Knopf Inc. Copyright by Kahlil Gibran and renewed 1951 by Administrators C.T.A. of the Kahlil Gibran Estate and Mary G. Gibran; ROBERT GRAVES, "At First Sight", from *Collected Poems 1975*. Reprinted with permission of A.P. Watt Ltd. on behalf of the Executors of the Estate of Robert Graves; CHARLOTTE GRAY, "Someone long parted ...", "Another Spring"; IRISH TOASTS, from *Slainté, your book of Irish Toasts and Irish Whiskey"*, © Copyright 1980, Irish Distillers Group PLC, reprinted with permission; HELEN KELLER, "Red-Letter Days" from *My Religion*. Reprinted courtesy of the Swedenborg Foundation, New York, NY 10010, copyright 1960, USA; JOHN D. MACDONALD, "When you don't edit yourself" from *Bright Orange For The Shroud*. Reprinted with permission of John Farquharson Ltd. and Alfred A. Knopf Inc; WAYNE MACKEY, quote from *The Oklahoma City Times*, copyright The Oklahoma Publishing Company; HENRY ALONZO MYERS, "Bound To Us In Triumph and Disaster". Reprinted from Henry Alonzo Myers: *Are Men Equal? An Inquiry into the Meaning of American Democracy*. © Copyright, 1945, by Henry Alonzo Myers. Used by permission of the publisher, Cornell University Press; WILLIAM STIDGER, "A Thanksgiving Letter". Reprinted with permission of Christian Advocate, Nashville, Tennessee 37202, USA.

PHOTOGRAPHS AND ILLUSTRATIONS:
ALTIORA, illustrating "A friend ...". From *Het Wonder Ligt in Jezelf*, published by Altiora, Belgium; CAMERA PRESS, illustrating "A Sorrow Shared"; DOVER PUBLICATIONS LTD, for pictures illustrating "Another Spring", "Friendship is ...", "A Particular Person Matters" and extract from "The Prophet"; ROBERT ESTALL, illustrating "Old Coats,

Old Friends"; RICHARD EXLEY, illustrating "Definitions of Friendship"; DALTON EXLEY, for front cover design, adapted from an illustration in *Art Nouveau Designs in Color,* Mucha et al, 1974 Dover Publications Inc, New York; MECKY FÖGELING, illustrating "Against all the Evils of Life"; FAX PHOTOS LTD, illustrating "Surprises from Devizes"; JOHN GARRETT, illustrating "Red Letter Days"; SYLVESTER JACOBS, illustrating pieces by Henry Alonzo Myers, Henry David Thoreau, "Small Service", "His thoughts were slow ...", "A Kind of Habit" and "He's Alive!"; HARRY LAPOW, illustrating extract by Richard Bach, "Annie and Edith" and "What is a Friend?". From *Coney Island Beach People.* Reprinted with permission of the Estate of Harry Lapow, Marcelle Lapow Toor, executrix; LISA MACKSON, illustrating "Without a word, without a sign"; PETER NEMETSCHEK, illustrating "People Need People". Copyright © Universal Features; BEN NICHOLSON, illustrating quote by Aristotle. © Angela Verren-Taunt. Reprinted with permission; FRED PLAUT, illustrating quote by Aesop; GEORGE RODGER, illustrating "No Man is an Island". Reprinted with permission of The John Hillelson Agency Limited; CLARE SCHWOB, illustrating "Day or Night"; BEN SHAH, illustrating extract by Leo Tolstoy. From *Prints and Posters of Ben Shah,* published by Dover Publications Inc, New York; W. EUGENE SMITH, illustrating "The Gift of Friendship". Reprinted with permission of The John Hillelson Agency Limited; ULRIKE WELSCH, illustrating words by Ouida, J.D. MacDonald and Shakespeare. From *The World I Love To See* © The Boston Globe. Photographs by Ulrike Welsch; ANS WESTRA, illustrating extract by Eliot and "You haven't changed at all!". From *Maori* by James Ritchie, published by A.H. & A.W. Reed, New Zealand; ZEFA PICTURE LIBRARY, illustrating extract by Angela Douglas.

Other gift books from Exley Publications
Love, a Keepsake. £5.99. Writers and poets old and new have captured the feeling of being in love, in this very personal collection. Specially designed as a lover's gift and bound in pale blue suedel. Gift-wrapped with sealing wax.
Love, a Celebration. £5.99. Bound in burgundy suedel, this is a gift for someone special in your life. A selection of poems and prose by great writers celebrate the joys and wonders of love. Gift-wrapped with sealing wax.
Marriage, a Keepsake. £5.99. With a silvery suedel cover, this collection of poems and prose contains some of the finest love messages between husbands and wives. For all couples from those about to marry to those who have known many good years together. Gift-wrapped with sealing wax.
For Mother, a gift of love. £5.99. Bound in dusky blue suedel, this collection of tributes to mothers includes such great writers such as Victor Hugo, Alfred Lord Tennyson and C. Day Lewis. A perfect gift for Mothering Sunday – or any other day! Gift-wrapped with sealing wax.
For Father, a gift of love. £5.99. Show your father how much you appreciate him with this thoughtfully compiled collection of poems and prose. Handsomely bound in brown suedel, this is something he will keep and treasure.
Love is a Grandmother. £5.99. "Everyone should have one, especially if you don't have television, because grandmothers are the only grown-ups who have the time!" Tributes from such great writers as Walter De La Mare, Hilaire Belloc and Bertram Russell for this anthology, bound in soft beige suedel. Gift-wrapped with sealing wax.

United Kingdom
Order these books from your local bookseller or from Exley Publications Ltd, Dept BP, 16 Chalk Hill, Watford, Herts WD1 4BN. (Please send £1.00 to cover post and packing.)
United States
All these titles are distributed in the United States by Slawson Communications Inc., 165 Vallecitos de Oro, San Marcos, CA 92069 and are priced at $8.95 each.